Ida

In Her Own Words

The timeless writings of
Ida B. Wells from 1893

Ida
In Her Own Words

*The timeless writings of
Ida B. Wells from 1893*

CLASS LEGISLATION

LYNCH LAW

Edited by Michelle Duster

BENJAMIN WILLIAMS PUBLISHING
WWW.BWPUBLISHING.COM

The images included are reproductions from the original pamphlet.

Cover photograph: Ida B. Wells in 1896.
Cover design by Cathy D. Reedy.

IDA: IN HER OWN WORDS

ISBN: 978-0-9802398-1-2

Printed in The United States of America
3rd Printing

Benjamin Williams Publishing
500 N. Michigan Ave., Suite 300
Chicago, Illinois 60611
www.bwpublishing.com

CONTENTS

CALL FOR THE BOYCOTT

SOME BACKGROUND AND CONTEXT

BY TROY DUSTER

In order to appreciate the focus and passion behind Ida B. Wells' decision to call for a boycott of the World's Fair of 1893 (the Columbian Exposition), it is important to understand the larger social context of the formative years of her life. Although born into slavery, emancipation occurred when she was a mere toddler. Her social and political consciousness – both from her early childhood and most certainly through her adolescent years – was seared indelibly during the period of Reconstruction (Giddings 2008; Harding 1983).

Slaves had been held back from learning to read

and write, and in some jurisdictions it was even a criminal offense for a white person to teach a slave to read. Once they had freedom, new communities of former slaves were bursting with energy and enthusiastic support for literacy, for as many as possible, and as fast as possible. Just after the Civil War, northern troops literally "occupied" the southern states of the defeated confederacy, and in the short space of a few years Blacks suddenly found themselves with a widespread and increasingly used right to vote, to officially marry, to own property, and of course, to attend school.

Education was seen as the key that would open many new doors, from employment to political and economic ascendancy. In this new South, Blacks were being elected to city councils, state legislatures, and to the U.S. Congress. This was also a period of northern missionary zeal to help the newly freed slaves, and the new schools were a beacon of hope that beckoned Christian women from the Northeast and Midwest. They came by the hundreds, even thousands, and in that first decade of Reconstruction the rates of literacy among Blacks skyrocketed. A sense of hopefulness, indeed, a trajectory that signaled eventual political and economic sovereignty seized the imagination of many – both young and old – but for none more fiercely than young Ida. From her childhood through her adolescence, she grew up in a climate in which it was taken for granted by those in her circle that social and political equality between the races would eventually be accomplished – if not in her lifetime, then certainly in a reasonable, even inexorably progressive direction into a foreseeable future.

What no one could have foreseen was the smoldering deal that would be struck between northern and southern whites in the Tilden-Hayes compromise. Eventually, this would mean the withdrawal of northern troops, the end of Reconstruction – and the ushering in of an era of unprecedented ascendancy of the ideas and practices of white supremacy. Ida bore witness to these changes, but never accepted that there could be a permanent erosion of the rule of a more

egalitarian law that she had experienced in her formative years. In large measure, this is the context in
which she refused to take a back seat to whites (or be
"escorted" to a separate and segregated section) in the
famous train episode. "White supremacy" was codi-
fied into specific laws (later called *Jim Crow laws*) after
Reconstruction, and the strict rules forbidding Blacks
to have equal access to travel accommodations on
trains was one of the many proliferations of these new
laws. If there is one moment in U.S. history where we
can trace the source of the scaffolding and architecture
of white supremacy via legislation, it would be to the
Supreme Court ruling in the *Dred Scott* decision.

During slavery, while the law said one thing, the
free states had variable practices and policies concern-
ing runaway slaves. In matters of strict law, from 1820
(the Missouri Compromise) to 1857 (the year of the
Dred Scott decision) once a slave crossed into a free
state, (s)he was "free." Indeed, when masters would
bring their slaves with them while traveling into a free
state, ardent abolitionists would sometimes confront

slaves in the service of their masters and inform them of their rights: that they were not fugitives, but legally entitled to their freedom. There was a hitch. One had to seek and secure that freedom through the courts.

The white population of the free states were typically against the expansion of slavery into new territories. However, this is not to suggest that the North was teeming with ardent abolitionists. Rather, northern whites rarely confronted slave-owners and slaves, except on those occasions when a southern businessman would vacation during the summer, and bring his slave(s) with him. Under these circumstances, when there was some contestation between the abolitionists, who were seen as "political" and even "radical," there was a decided tendency for the population to side with the slave-owners. The border states were precisely that, in between, not just geographically, but ideologically and politically.

Such was the context for the case of Dred Scott, a house-servant and slave to a Missouri land-owner. Scott had accompanied his master, who was also an officer in the United States Army, to a northern state where slavery was illegal. According to the Missouri Compromise of 1820, living in a territory declared free of slavery (as explicitly stated in that Compromise) entitled a slave to free status. Abolitionists assisted Scott in a lawsuit to win his freedom. There ensued a protracted legal battle that would flurry, then languished in the courts for more than a decade, inching its way through the lower courts. In March, 1857, the Supreme Court issued its ruling in the *Dred Scott* decision, that the Missouri Compromise was unconstitutional because Congress had no authority "to deprive white citizens of their right to enjoy Black property north of the Missouri line." (Harding, 1983: 202).

The *Dred Scott* decision rested on two issues critical to the status of both slaves and free Blacks. First, it answered the question: did a slave have the right to sue for his or her freedom? Here was how Chief Justice Roger Taney posed the matter:

> Can a negro, whose ancestors were
> imported into this country, and sold as

slaves, become a member of the political community, formed and brought into existence by the Constitution of the United States, and as such become entitled to all rights, and privileges, and immunities, guaranteed by that instrument to the citizen? One of which rights is the privilege of suing in a court of the United States in the cases specified in the Constitution? (Harding, 1983: 201)

Justice Taney wrote explicitly, that "we the people" was never intended to include Blacks, slave nor free. He had said in 1831, and then repeated in his 1857 Supreme Court ruling, that the Constitution, the Courts at every level, the federal government, and the States, all routinely denied Blacks equal access to rights of citizenship, and that "neither Dred Scott nor any other person of African descent had any citizenship rights which were binding on white

American society" (Harding, 1983: 201).

The law, and the courts which interpreted the law in that period, determined that it was a crime for a slave to run away -- and that "negroes had no rights to sue for redress" in 1857. There are many reasons why the nation moved to Civil War, and no one can claim the singular importance of any one of those reasons. But one thing historians often note is that the impact of the *Dred Scott* decision reverberated in ways that were completely unanticipated. For example, before *Dred Scott*, free Blacks living outside the South (and even some within southern states) could believe that their freedoms were guaranteed by the law. Now, with the new Supreme Court decision, even free Blacks were jolted into a new consciousness, namely, that their rights to property, political position and education were subject to "white supremacy."

From 1865 to 1872, a federal agency, the Bureau of Refugees, Freedmen, and Abandoned Lands, played an important role in supporting the education of newly freed slaves. That agency provided resources for the burgeoning schools, and in turn drew the ire of white Southerners who saw this as a major threat to their control of the Black population. After the assassination of President Abraham Lincoln in 1865, they successfully lobbied the new president, Andrew Johnson, to abandon programs and projects of the new agency, ultimately crippling it by the early 1870s. But the ultimate blow to Black aspirations would come in the aftermath of the bitter 1876 presidential election, in which there was no clear winner between the Republican, Rutherford Hayes, and the Democrat, Samuel Tilden. The result was the famous Tilden-Hayes compromise of 1877, in which the North agreed to withdraw federal troops – and effectively, end Reconstruction. While there had certainly been widespread intimidation and violence directed against Blacks in those first twelve years after Emancipation, it would pale in comparison to the unleashing of white supremacist fury by newly emboldened groups such as the Ku Klux Klan after 1877. But it was not just the vigilante groups, it was the omnipresent feature of Jim

Crow laws that began to penetrate every aspect of life between the races. In the next decades, laws would appear that forbade Blacks from using the same public restrooms as whites, from eating in the same public spaces with whites, from sitting in audiences at theaters with whites, and of course, from riding in the same public transit vehicles and attending schools with whites.

Post-Reconstruction
(Precursor to the Columbian
Exposition Exclusion of Blacks)

There were certainly abolitionists in the early nineteenth century – and also more "neutral" legal scholars who were aghast at the Supreme Court's ruling on the Missouri Compromise as little more than the extension of the legitimacy of slavery into non-slave states. But slavery as a dominant social institution, and the particularized enslavement of Blacks deeply penetrated the fabric of social life in America. Whites came to own legal status privilege as whites, and this sense of ownership was increasingly experienced as normal and natural (Roediger, 1992; Harris, 1994; Allen, 1995).

Oliver Wendell Holmes, however much he can be appropriately credited with refining and in some ways, redefining an important segment of legal thinking, also very much adopted the epistemological frame of his era. Holmes' legal realism was couched in a strong acceptance of the progressive era's trumpeting of a newfound rationality in the study of history, science, and economics -- with a heavy emphasis upon evolutionary thinking in all of these realms (White, 1993: 112-116). Holmes, writing on the contextual nature of medical information in a court of law, stated:

> We may express a doubt whether doctors would regard a work on 'medical jurisprudence' as a sufficient handbook of science; and we are very confident that few lawyers would feel strongly bound by its opinions on a point of law. (A lawyer)...wants to know

under what circumstances the courts have admitted (a medical) defense (such as insanity) in a criminal action. (White, 1993: 115)

Most important for this line of reasoning was Holmes' heavy reliance on the work of Henry Maine's *Ancient Law*, and its evolutionary theory of social change. It was this extraordinarily powerful and influential work that shaped Holmes' view that legal doctrines come into being "for contextual reasons." Following Maine, Holmes noted that times change, and the body of principles that evolved in an earlier time ossify and become irrelevant, maladaptive, possibly even destructive if resurrected. But Holmes would be presented with a case that captured all the elements of his theory of jurisprudence and its relationship to social change, that would challenge the core assumptions.

A practice emerged in the post-Reconstruction South that bore striking similarity to indentured servitude for Blacks -- a turning back of the clock to ensure state-mandated, state-coerced cheap labor from Blacks. It was called the criminal-surety arrangement. Several southern states had laws that permitted those convicted of minor offenses to either pay fines, or enter into agreements to work for a specified period of time. (It was used almost exclusively against Blacks, and sometimes even serious crimes were reduced to lesser charges just so the criminal-surety arrangement could be invoked.)[1] If the person did not serve out the full time, (s)he could be convicted again, to work for the full amount of time allotted in the original agreement.

At the turn of the century, a case would make its way to the Supreme Court that would reshape this new conflation of criminality with "indentured" status. A man named Ed Rivers pled guilty to petit larceny, and was unable to come up with the fine of $58.75. Rivers entered into an agreement with a J. A. Reynolds to work for nine months and 24 days. Rivers subsequently quit, was picked up, fined, and when he could not pay the fine, it was paid by another employer, who demanded in return that Rivers work for him for 14

[1] c.f. R. S. Baker (1964)

months, at $6 per month. This case ended up in the Supreme Court, because the Justice Department used the case to challenge the constitutionality of criminal-surety under the Thirteenth Amendment.

In the *United States v Reynolds* (1914), the Supreme Court unanimously rejected the Justice Department's challenge, and upheld the constitutionality of the criminal-surety arrangement. Oliver Wendell Holmes was a member of that Court, and he vigorously defended criminal-surety. The position which Holmes adopted in this case can not be explained by examining the analytically coherent, legal intellectual arguments which he had assumed over his full career in jurisprudence. Rather, Holmes' ruling on criminal-surety can best be explained by the *Zeitgeist* -- the simultaneous over-arching climate and deeply rooted domain assumptions in the subtle and seamless social continuity from slavery to wage labor. There was in this case, and the series of legal cases that sprung from it, the inter-lacing of law with science and (at the time) the evolutionary theories of how social change should develop. Holmes had railed against the power of Social Darwinism and its hold upon the courts, but he himself was swept away by it in ways that are only now fully appreciated (White, 1993).

While the ultimate Supreme decision *United States v Reynolds* would finally come down a full decade after the Columbian Exposition, the practices of criminal-surety were deeply embedded, endemic and well understood for the last two decades of the nineteenth century. Ida B. Wells bore witness to these developments, but not silently, and never with assent. She had, after all, implored Blacks to leave the South when they could not count on the courts to guarantee their safety, much less achieve equality or expect justice. Her early call for Blacks to boycott white establishments in Memphis was a harbinger of her later call for Blacks to boycott the World's Fair in 1893. There was thus consistency, coherence and continuity in her political strategies. For example, she had toured England to get allies in the United Kingdom to boycott cotton from the American South, so long as the practice of lynching was condoned, by its ominous silence, by the federal government. When even Oliver Wendell Holmes, the most respected and revered "Justice" on the Supreme Court could turn his back on the transparently supreme injustice of criminal-surety, one can clearly understand the social and political climate of Wells' call for a direct-action boycott.

About the Pamphlet

Class Legislation and *Lynch Law* were originally sections of a pamphlet entitled *The Reason Why the Colored American is not in the World's Columbian Exposition: The Afro-American's Contribution to Columbian Literature.* Ida B. Wells, along with Frederick Douglass, Irvine Garland Penn and Ferdinand L. Barnett (whom Ida later married) were the four contributors to the pamphlet.

Thousands of pamphlets were printed and distributed at the entrance of the 1893 Columbian Exposition, which took place in Chicago, Illinois. People from all over the United States, as well as the rest of the world, came to the Exposition to enjoy the festivities and marvel at the innovations unveiled. Ida B. Wells and supporters felt this was a perfect opportunity to have a wide audience for outsiders to become aware of the injustice and horrors that were taking place in the same country that boasted such a wonderful festival.

Editor's Note:

The original pamphlet, printed in 1893, was produced in haste. There were some mistakes in the text that appear to be typos. In addition, some of the conventions of the English language have changed since the turn of the 20th century. In order to maintain the integrity and authenticity of the work, the text, with minor exceptions, has been reproduced with the spellings and punctuation as it was originally printed.

The Reason Why

the Colored American

is not in the World's

Columbian Exposition.

The Afro-American's Contribution

to Columbian Literature.

Ida B Wells

Chicago

July 1893.

TO THE PUBLIC.

This pamphlet is published by contribution from colored people of the United States. The haste necessary for the press, prevents the incorporation of interesting data showing the progress of the colored people in commercial lines.

Besides the cuts of a school and hospital it was desired to have a cut of the Capital Savings Bank, a flourishing institution conducted by the colored people of Washington, D. C. The cut, however, did not arrive in time for the press.

Twenty thousand copies of THE REASON WHY are now ready for gratuitous distribution. Applications by mail will enclose three cents for postage. All orders addressed to the undersigned will be promptly acknowledged.   IDA B. WELLS,

Room 9, 128 Clark St.,

AUGUST 30, 1893.   Chicago, Ill.

THE REASON WHY

The Colored American is not in the World's Columbian Exposition.

The Afro-American's Contribution to Columbian Literature

Copies sent to any address on receipt of three cents for postage. Address MISS IDA B. WELLS, 128 S. Clark Street, Chicago, Ill.. U. S. A.

CLASS LEGISLATION

[ATTRIBUTED TO IDA B. WELLS]

The Civil War of 1861-5 ended slavery. It left us free, but it also left us homeless, penniless, ignorant, nameless and friendless. Life is derived from the earth, and the American Government is thought to be more humane than the Russian. Russia's liberated serf was given three acres of land and agricultural implements with which to begin his career of liberty and independence. But to us no foot of land nor implement was given. We were turned loose to starvation, destitution and death. So desperate was our condition that some of our statesmen declared it useless to try to save us by legislation as we were doomed to extinction.

The original fourteen slaves which the Dutch ship landed at Jamestown, Virginia in 1619, had increased to four millions by 1865, and were mostly in the southern states. We were liberated not only empty-handed but left in the power of a people who resented our emancipation as an act of unjust punishment to them. They were therefore armed with a motive for doing everything in their power to render our freedom a curse rather than a blessing. In the halls of National legislation the Negro was made a free man and citizen. The southern states, which had seceded from the Union before the war, regained their autonomy by accepting these amendments and promising to support the constitution. Since "reconstruction" these amendments have been largely nullified in the south, and the Negro vote reduced from a majority to a cipher. This has been accomplished by political massacres, by midnight outrages of Ku Klux Klans, and by state legislative enactment. That the legislation of the white south is hostile to the interests of our race is shown by the existence in most of the southern states of the convict lease system, the chain-gang, vagrant laws, election frauds, keeping back laborers wages, paying for work in worthless script instead of lawful money, refusing to sell land to Negroes and the many political massacres where hundreds of black men were murdered for the crime (?) of casting the ballot. These were some of the means resorted to during our first years of liberty to defeat the little beneficence comprehended in the act of our emancipation.

The South is enjoying to-day the results of this course pursued for the first fifteen years of our freedom. The Solid South means that the South is a unit for white supremacy, and that the Negro is practically disfranchised through intimidation. The large Negro population of that section gives the South thirty-nine more votes in the National Electoral College which elects the President of the United States, than she would otherwise have. These votes are cast by white men who represent the Democratic Party, while the Negro vote has heretofore represented the entire

Republican Party of the South. Every National Congress has thirty-nine more white members from the South in the House of Representatives than there would be, were it not for the existence of her voiceless and unrepresented Negro vote and population. One Representative is allowed to every 150,000 persons. What other States have usurped, Mississippi made in 1892, a part of her organic law.

The net result of the registration under the educational and poll tax provision of the new Mississippi Constitution is as follows.

Over 21 years.		Registered votes.
Whites – – –	110,100	68,127
Negroes – –	147,205	8,615
Total – – –	257,305	76,742

In 1880 there were 130,278 colored voters a colored majority of 22,024. Every county in Mississippi now has a white majority. Thirty-three counties have less than 100 Negro votes.

Yazoo county, with 6,000 Negroes of voting age, has only nine registered votes, or one to each 666. Noxubee has four colored voters or one to each 150 colored men. In Lowndes there is one colored voter to each 310 men. In the southern tier counties on the Gulf about one Negro man in eight or ten is registered, which is the best average.

Depriving the Negro of his vote leaves the entire political, legislative, executive and judicial machinery of the country in the hands of the white people. The religious, moral and financial forces of the country are also theirs. This power has been used to pass laws forbidding intermarriage between the races, thus fostering immorality. The union, which the law forbids, goes on without its sanction in dishonorable alliances.

Sec. 3291 M. & V. Code Tennessee, provides that: The intermarriage of white persons with Negroes, Mulattoes or persons of mixed blood descended from a Negro to the third generation inclusive, or their living together as man and wife in this State, is hereby forbidden.

Sec. 3292, M. & V. Code, Tenn., provides that: The persons knowingly violating the provisions in above Section shall be deemed guilty of a felony, and upon conviction thereof shall undergo imprisonment in the penitentiary not less than one nor more than five years; and the court may, in the event of conviction, on the recommendation of the jury, substitute in lieu of punishment in the penitentiary, fine and imprisonment in the county jail.

NOTES: – It need not charge the act to have been done knowingly. Such persons may be indicted for living together as man and wife, though married in another state where such marriages are lawful. 7 Bok. 9. This law is constitutional. 3 Hill's 287.

Out of 44 states only twenty-three states and territories allow whites and Negroes to marry if they see fit to contract such alliances, viz: Louisiana, Illinois, Kansas, Connecticut, Iowa, Maine, Massachusetts, Michigan, Minnesota, Montana, New Hampshire, New Jersey, New York, North Dakota, Ohio, Oklahoma, Pennsylvania, Rhode Island, South Dakota, Vermont, Washington, Wisconsin, and Wyoming. All of these are northern states and territories except one – Louisiana.

The others, especially Virginia, Maryland, W. Virginia, Delaware, North Carolina, South Carolina, Georgia, Florida, Alabama, Mississippi, Arkansas, Kentucky, Missouri, Indiana, Tennessee, and Texas, have laws similar to the Tennessee Statute. Under these laws men and women are prosecuted and punished in the courts of these states for inter-marrying, but not for unholy alliances.

"The Thirteenth amendment to the Constitution making the race citizens, was virtually made null and void by the legislatures of the re-constructed states. So it became necessary to pass the Civil Rights Bill giving colored people the right to enter public places and ride on first-class railroad cars." – Johnson's History of the Negro race in America. This Bill passed Congress in 1875. For nearly ten years it was the Negro's only protection in the south. In 1884 the United States Supreme Court declared the Civil Rights Bill unconstitutional. With "state's rights', doctrine once more supreme and this last barrier removed, the southern states are enacting separate car laws. Mississippi, Louisiana, Texas, Arkansas, Tennessee, Alabama Georgia and Kentucky have each passed a law making it punishable by fine and imprisonment for colored persons to ride in the same railway carriage with white persons unless as servants to white passengers. These laws have all been passed within the past 6 years. Kentucky passed this law last year (1892). The legislatures of Missouri, West Virginia and North Carolina had such bills under consideration at the sessions this year, but they were defeated.

Aside from the inconsistency of class legislation in this country, the cars for colored persons are rarely equal in point of accommodation. Usually one-half the smoking car is reserved for the "colored car." Many times only a cloth curtain or partition run half way up, divides this "colored car" from the smoke, obscene language and foul air of the smokers' end of the coach. Into this "separate but equal (?)" half-carriage are crowded all classes and conditions of Negro humanity, without regard to sex, standing, good breeding, or ability to pay for better accommodation. White men pass through these "colored cars" and ride in them whenever they feel inclined to do so, but no colored woman however refined, well educated or well dressed may ride in the ladies, or first-class coach, in any of these states unless she is a nurse-maid traveling with a white child. The railroad fare is exactly the same in all cases however. There is no redress at the hands of the law. The men who execute the law share the same prejudices as those who made these laws, and the courts rule in favor of the law. A colored young school teacher was dragged out of the only ladies coach on the train in Tennessee by the conductor and two trainmen. She entered suit in the state courts as directed by the United States Supreme Court. The Supreme Court of the State of Tennessee, although the lower courts had awarded damages to the plaintiff, reversed the decision of those courts and ruled that the smoking car into which the railway employees tried to force the plaintiff was a first-class car, equal in every respect to the one in which she was seated, and as she was violating the law, she was not entitled to damages.

The Tennessee law is as follows,

—— Chapter 52 —— Page 135 —An Act to promote the comfort of passengers on railroad trains by regulating separate accommodations for the white and colored races.

SECTION 1. Be it enacted by the General Assembly of the State of Tennessee – That all railroads carrying passengers in the State (other than street railroads) shall provide equal but separate accommodations for the white and colored races, by providing two or more passenger cars for each passenger train, or by dividing the passenger cars by a partition so as to secure separate accommodations; PROVIDED, that any person may be permitted to take a nurse in the car or compartment set aside for such persons; PROVID- ED, that this Act shall not apply to mixed and freight trains which only carry one passenger or combination passenger and baggage; PROVIDED, always that in such cases the one passenger car so carried shall be partitioned into apartments, one apartment for the whites and one for the colored.

SEC. 2.   Be it further enacted: That the conduc- tors of such passenger trains shall have power and are hereby required to assign to the car or compartments of the car (when it is divided by a partition) used for the race to which such passengers belong, and should any passenger refuse to occupy the car to which he or she is assigned by such conductor, said conductor shall have power to refuse to carry such passenger on his train, and for such neither he nor the railroad com- pany shall be liable for any damages in any court in this State.

SEC. 3.   Be it further enacted: That all railroad companies that shall fail, refuse or neglect to comply with the requirements of section 1, of this Act shall be deemed guilty of a misdemeanor, and, upon conviction in a court of competent jurisdiction, be fined not less than one hundred, nor more than four hundred dollars, and any conductor that shall fail; neglect or refuse to carry out the provisions of this Act shall, upon conviction, be fined not less than twenty-five, nor more than fifty dollars for each offense.

SEC. 4. Be it further enacted: That this Act take effect ninety days from and after its passage, the public welfare requiring it.

Passed March 11, 1891.

THOMAS R. MYERS.

Speaker of the House of Representatives.

Approved March 27, 1891.   W. C. DISMUKES,

Speaker of Senate

JOHN P. BUCHANAN,

Governor.

LYNCH LAW

BY IDA B. WELLS.

"**L**ynch Law," says the *Virginia Lancet*, "as known by the appellation, had its origin in 1780 in a combination of citizens of Pittsylvania County, Virginia, entered into for the purpose of suppressing a trained band of horse-thieves and counterfeiters whose well concocted schemes had bidden defiance to the ordinary laws of the land, and whose success encouraged and emboldened them in their outrages upon the community. Col. Wm. Lynch drafted the constitution for this combination of citizens, and hence "Lynch Law" has ever since been the name given to the summary infliction of punishment by private and uuauthorized citizens."

This law continues in force to-day in some of the oldest states of the Union, where courts of justice have long been established, whose laws are executed by white Americans. It flourishes most largely in the states which foster the convict lease system, and is brought to bear mainly, against the Negro. The first fifteen years of his freedom he was murdered by masked mobs for trying to vote. Public opinion having made lynching for that cause unpopular, a new reason is given to justify the murders of the past 15 years. The Negro was first charged with attempting to rule white people, and hundreds were murdered on that pretended supposition. He is now charged with assaulting or attempting to assault white women. This charge, as false as it is foul, robs us of the sympathy of the world and is blasting the race's good name.

The men who make these charges encourage or lead the mobs which do the lynching. They belong to the race which holds Negro life cheap, which owns the telegraph wires, newspapers, and all other communication with the outside world. They write the reports which justify lynching by painting the Negro as black as possible, and those reports are accepted by the press associations and the world without question or investigation. The mob spirit has increased with alarming frequency and violence. Over a thousand black men, women and children have been thus sacrificed the past ten years. Masks have long since been thrown aside and the lynchings of the present day take place in broad daylight. The sheriffs, police and state officials stand by and see the work well done. The coroner's jury is often formed among those who took part in the lynching and a verdict, "Death at the hands of parties unknown to the jury" is rendered. As the number of lynchings have increased, so has the cruelty and barbarism of the lynchers. Three human beings was burned alive in civilized America during the first six months of this year (1893). Over one hundred have been lynched in this half year. They were hanged, then cut, shot and burned.

The following table published by the Chicago *Tribune* January, 1892, is submitted for thoughtful consideration.

1882, 52	Negroes murdered by mobs		
1883, 39	"	"	" "
1884, 53	"	"	" "
1885, 77	"	"	" "
1886, 73	"	"	" "
1887, 70	"	"	" "
1888, 72	"	"	" "
1889, 95	"	"	" "
1890, 100	"	"	" "
1891, 169	"	"	" "

Of this number

269	were charged with rape.			
253	"	"	"	murder
44	"	"	"	robbery.
37	"	"	"	incendiarism.
4	"	"	"	burglary.
27	"	"	"	race prejudice.

13 were charged with quarreling with white men.

10 "   "   "   making threats.

7 "   "   "   rioting.

5 "   "   "   miscegenation.

32 "   "   "   no reasons given.

This table shows (1) that only one-third of nearly a thousand murdered black persons have been even charged with the crime of outrage. This crime is only so punished when white women accuse black men, which accusation is never proven. The same crime committed by Negroes against Negroes, or by white men against black women is ignored even in the law courts.

(2) That nearly as many were lynched for murder as for the above crime, which the world believes is the cause of all the lynchings. The world affects to believe that *white* womanhood and childhood, surrounded by their lawful protectors, are not safe in the neighborhood of the black man, who protected and cared for them during the four years of civil war. The husbands,

fathers and brothers of those white women were away for four years, fighting to keep the Negro in slavery, yet not one case of assault has ever been reported!

(3) That "robbery, incendiarism, race prejudice, quarreling with white men, making threats, rioting, miscegenation (marrying a white person), and burglary," are capital offenses punishable by death when committed by a black against a white person. Nearly as many blacks were lynched for these charges (and unproven) as for the crime of rape.

(4) That for nearly fifty of these lynchings no reason is given. There is no demand for reasons, or need of concealment for what no one is held responsible. The simple word of any white person against a Negro is sufficient to get a crowd of white men to lynch a Negro. Investigation as to the guilt or innocence of the accused is never made. Under these conditions, white men have only to blacken their faces, commit crimes against the peace of the community, accuse some Negro, nor rest till he is killed by a mob. Will Lewis, an 18 year old Negro youth was lynched at Tullahoma,

Tennessee, August 1891, for being "drunk and saucy to white folks."

The women of the race have not escaped the fury of the mob. In Jackson, Tennessee, in the summer of 1886, a white woman died of poisoning. Her black cook was suspected, and as a box of rat poison was found in her room, she was hurried away to jail. When the mob had worked itself to the lynching pitch, she was dragged out of jail, every stitch of clothing torn from her body, and she was hung in the public court-house square in sight of everybody. Jackson is one of the oldest towns in the State, and the State Supreme Court holds its sittings there; but no one was arrested for the deed – not even a protest was uttered. The husband of the poisoned woman has since died a raving maniac, and his ravings showed that he, and not the poor black cook, was the poisoner of his wife. A fifteen year old Negro girl was hanged in Rayville, Louisiana, in the spring of 1892, on the same charge of poisoning white persons. There was no more proof or investigation of this case than the one in Jackson. A

Negro woman, Lou Stevens, was hanged from a railway bridge in Hollendale, Mississippi, in 1892. She was charged with being accessory to the murder of her white paramour, who had shamefully abused her.

In 1892 there were 241 persons lynched. The entire number is divided among the following states.

Alabama	22	Montana	4
Arkansas	25	New York	1
California	3	North Carolina	5
Florida	11	North Dakota	1
Georgia	17	Ohio	3
Idaho	8	South Carolina	5
Illinois	1	Tennessee	28
Kansas	3	Texas	15
Kentucky	9	Virginia	7
Louisiana	29	West Virginia	5
Maryland	1	Wyoming	9
Mississippi	16	Arizona Ter.	3
Missouri	6	Oklahoma	2

Of this number 160 were of Negro descent. Four of them were lynched in New York, Ohio and Kansas; the remainder were murdered in the south. Five of this number were females. The charges for which they were lynched cover a wide range. They are as follows:

Rape	–	46	Attempted Rape –	11
Murder	–	58	Suspected Robbery	4
Rioting	–	3	Larceny –	1
Race prejudice	–	6	Self-defense –	1
No cause given	–	4	Insulting women –	2
Incendiarism	–	6	Desperadoes –	6
Robbery –	–	6	Fraud – –	1
Assault and Battery		1	Attempted murder	2
	No offense stated, boy and girl –			2

In the case of the boy and girl above referred to, their father, named Hastings, was accused of the murder of a white man; his fourteen year old daughter and sixteen year old son were hanged and their bodies filled with bullets, then the father was also lynched.

This was in November, 1892, at Jonesville, Louisiana.

A lynching equally as cold-blooded took place in Memphis, Tennessee, March 1892. Three young colored men in an altercation at their place of business, fired on white men in self-defense. They were imprisoned for three days, then taken out by the mob and horribly shot to death. Thomas Moss, Will Stewart and Calvin McDowell, were energetic business men who had built up a flourishing grocery business. This business had prospered and that of a rival white grocer named Barrett had declined. Barrett led the attack on their grocery which resulted in the wounding of three white men. For this cause were three innocent men barbarously lynched, and their families left without protectors. Memphis is one of the leading cities of Tennessee, a town of seventy-five thousand inhabitants! No effort whatever was made to punish the murderers of these three men. It counted for nothing that the victims of this outrage were three of the best known young men of a population of thirty thousand colored people of Memphis. They were the officers of the company which conducted the grocery. Moss being the President, Stewart the Secretary of the Company and McDowell the Manager. Moss was in the Civil Service of the United States as letter carrier, and all three were men of splendid reputation for honesty, integrity and sobriety. But their murderers, though well known, have never been indicted, were not even troubled with a preliminary examination.

With law held in such contempt, it is not a matter of surprise that the same city – one of the so-called queen cities of the South, should again give itself over to a display of almost indescribable barbarism. This time the mob made no attempt to conceal its identity, but reveled in the contemplation of its feast of crime. Lee Walker, a colored man was the victim. Two white women complained that while driving to town, a colored man jumped from a place of concealment and dragged one of the two women from the wagon, but their screams frightened him away. Alarm was given that a Negro had made an attempted assault upon the women and bands of men set out to run him down.

They shot a colored man who refused to stop when called. It was fully ten days before Walker was caught. He admitted that he did attack the women, but that he made no attempt to assault them; that he offered them no indecency whatever, of which as a matter of fact, they never accused him. He said he was hungry and he was determined to have something to eat, but after throwing one of the women out of the wagon, became frightened and ran away. He was duly arrested and taken to the Memphis jail. The fact that he was in prison and could be promptly tried and punished did not prevent the good citizens of Memphis from taking the law in their own hands, and Walker was lynched.

The *Memphis Commercial* of Sunday, July 23, contains a full account of the tragedy from which the following extracts are made.

At 12 o'clock last night, Lee Walker, who attempted to outrage Miss Mollie McCadden, last Tuesday morning, was taken from the county jail and hanged to a telegraph pole just north of the prison. All day rumors were afloat that with nightfall an attack would be made upon the jail, and as everyone anticipated that a vigorous resistance would be made, a conflict between the mob and the authorities was feared.

At 10 o'clock Capt. O'Haver, Sergt. Horan and several patrol men were on hand, but they could do nothing with the crowd. An attack by the mob was made on the door in the south wall and it yielded. Sheriff McLendon and several of his men threw themselves into the breach, but two or three of the storming party shoved by. They were seized by the police but were not subdued, the officers refraining from using their clubs. The entire mob might at first have been dispersed by ten policemen who would use their clubs, but the sheriff insisted that no violence be done.

The mob got an iron rail and used it as a battering ram against the lobby doors. Sheriff McLendon tried to stop them, and some one of the mob knocked him down with a chair. Still he counseled moderation and would not order his deputies and the police to disperse the crowd by force. The pacific policy of the sheriff impressed the mob with the idea that the officers were afraid, or at least would do them no harm, and they redoubled their efforts, urged on by a big switchman. At 12 o'clock the door of the prison was broken in with a rail.

As soon as the rapist was brought out of the door, calls were heard for a rope; then some one shouted "Burn him!" But there was no time to make a fire. When Walker got into the lobby a dozen of the men began beaten and stabbing him. He was half dragged, half carried to the corner of Front street and the alley between Sycamore and Mill, and hung to a telephone pole.

Walker made a desperate resistance. Two men entered his cell first and ordered him to come forth. He refused and they failing to drag him out, others entered. He scratched and bit his assailants, wounding several of them severely with his teeth. The mob retaliated by striking and cutting him with fists and knives. When he reached the steps leading down to the door he made another stand and was stabbed again and again. By the time he reached the lobby his power to resist was gone, and he was shoved along through the mob of yelling, cursing men and boys, who beat, spat upon and slashed the wretch-like demon. One of the leaders of the mob fell, and the crowd walked ruthlessly over him. He was badly hurt – a jawbone fractured and internal injuries inflicted. After the lynching friends took charge of him.

The mob proceeded north on Front street with the victim, stopping at Sycamore street to get a rope from a grocery. "Take him to the iron bridge on Main street," yelled several men. The men who had hold of the Negro were in a hurry to finish the job, however, and when they reached the telephone pole at the corner of Front street and the first alley north of Sycamore they stopped. A hastily improvised noose was slipped over the Negro's head and several young men mounted a pile of lumber near the pole and threw the rope over one of the iron stepping pins. The Negro was lifted up until his feet were three feet above the ground, the rope was made taut, and a corpse dangled in midair. A big fellow who helped lead the mob pulled the Negro's legs until his neck cracked. The wretch's clothes had been torn off, and, as he swung, the man who pulled his legs mutilated the corpse.

One or two knife cuts, more or less, made little difference in the appearance of the dead rapist, however, for before the rope was around his neck his skin was cut almost to ribbons. One pistol shot was fired while the corpse was hanging. A dozen voices protested against the use of firearms, and there was no more shooting. The body was permitted to hang for half an hour, then it was cut down and the rope divided among those who lingered around the scene of the tragedy. Then it was suggested that the corpse be burned, and it was done. The entire performance, from the assault on the jail to the burning of the dead Negro was witnessed by a score or so of policemen and as many deputy sheriffs, but not a hand was lifted to stop the proceedings after the jail door yielded.

As the body hung to the telegraph pole, blood streaming down from the knife wounds in his neck, his hips and lower part of his legs also slashed with knives, the crowd hurled expletives at him, swung the body so that it was dashed against the pole, and, so far from the ghastly sight proving trying to the nerves, the crowd looked on with complaisance, if not with real pleasure. The Negro died hard. The neck was not broken, as the body was drawn up without being given a fall, and death came by strangulation. For fully ten minutes after he was strung up the chest heaved occasionaly and there were convulsive movements of the limbs. Finally he was pronounced dead, and a few minutes later Detective Richardson climbed on a pile of staves and cut the rope. The body fell in a ghastly heap, and the crowd laughed at the sound and crowded around the prostrate body, a few kicking the inanimate carcass.

Detective Richardson, who is also a deputy coroner, then proceeded to impanel the following jury of inquest J. S. Moody, A. C. Waldran, B. J. Childs, J. N. House, Nelson Bills, T. L. Smith, and A. Newhouse. After viewing the body the inquest was adjourned without any testimony being taken until 9 o'clock this morning. The jury will meet at the coroner's office, 51 Beale street, upstairs, and decide on a verdict. If no witnesses are forthcoming, the jury will be able to arrive at a verdict just the same, as all members of it saw the lynching. Then some one raised the cry of "Burn him!" It was quickly taken up and soon resounded from a hundred throats. Detective Richardson for a long time, single handed, stood the crowd off. He talked and begged the men not to bring disgrace on the city by burning the body, arguing that all the vengeance possible had been wrought.

While this was going on a small crowd was busy starting a fire in middle of the street. The material was handy. Some bundles of staves were taken from the adjoining lumber yard for kindling. Heavier wood was obtained from the same source, and coal oil from a neighboring grocery. Then the cries of "Burn him! Burn him!" were redoubled.

Half a dozen men seized the naked body. The crowd cheered. They marched to the fire, and giving the body a swing, it was landed in the middle of the fire. There was a cry for more wood, as the fired had begun to die owing to the long delay. Willing hands procured the wood, and it was piled up on the Negro, almost, for a time, obscuring him from view. The head was in plain view, as also were the limbs, and one arm which stood out high above the body, the elbow crooked, held in that position by a stick of wood. In a few moments the hands began to swell, then came great blisters over all the exposed parts of the body; then in places the flesh was burned away and the bones began to show through. It was a horrible sight, one which perhaps none there had ever witnessed before. It proved too much for a large part of the crowd and the majority of the mob left very shortly after the burning began.

But a large number stayed, and were not a bit set back by the sight of a human body being burned to ashes. Two or three white women, accompanied by their escorts, pushed to the front to obtain an unobstructed view, and looked on with astonishing coolness and nonchalance. One man and woman brought a little girl, not over 12 years old, apparently their daughter, to view a scene which was calculated to drive sleep from the child's eyes for many nights, if not to produce a permanent injury to her nervous system. The comments of the crowd were varied. Some remarked on the efficacy of this style of cure for rapists, others rejoiced that men's wives and daughters were now safe from this wretch.

Some laughed as the flesh cracked and blistered, and while a large number pronounced the burning of a dead body as an useless episode, not in all that throng was a word of sympathy heard for the wretch himself.

The rope that was used to hang the Negro, and also that which was used to lead him from the jail, were eagerly sought by relic hunters. They almost fought for a chance to cut off a piece of rope, and in an incredably short time both ropes had disappeared and were scattered in the pockets of the crowd in sections of from an inch to six inches long. Others of the relic hunters remained until the ashes cooled to obtain such ghastly relics as the teeth, nails, and bits of charred skin of the immolated victim of his own lust. After burning the body the mob tied a rope around the charred trunk and dragged it down Main street to the court house, where it was hanged to a center pole. The rope broke and the corpse dropped with a thud, but it was again hoisted, the charred legs barely touching the ground. The teeth were

knocked out and the finger nails cut off as sou-
venirs. The crowd made so much noise that the
police interfered. Undertaker Walsh was tele-
phoned for, who took charge of the body and carried it to his establishment, where it will be prepared for burial in the potter's field today.

A prelude to this exhibition of 19th century barbarism was the following telegram received by the
Chicago *Inter-Ocean* at 2 o'clock, Saturday afternoon –
ten hours before the lynching:

"MEMPHIS, TENN, July 22, To *Inter-Ocean*, Chicago.
Lee Walker, colored man, accused of raping white women,
in jail here, will be taken out and burned by whites to-night.
Can you send Miss Ida Wells to write it up?
Answer. R. M. Martin, with Public Ledger."

The *Public Ledger* is one of the oldest evening
daily papers in Memphis, and this telegram shows that
the intentions of the mob were well known long before
they were executed. The personnel of the mob is given

by the Memphis *Appeal-Avalanche*. It says, "At first it seemed as if a crowd of roughs were the principals, but as it increased in size, men in all walks of life figured as leaders, although the majority were young men."

This was the punishment meted out to a Negro, charged, not with rape, but attempted assault, and without any proof as to his guilt, for the women were not given a chance to identify him. It was only a little less horrible than the burning alive of Henry Smith, at Paris, Texas, February 1st, 1893, or that of Edward Coy, in Texarkana, Texas, February 20, 1892. Both were charged with assault on white women, and both were tied to the stake and burned while yet alive, in the presence of ten thousand persons. In the case of Coy, the white woman in the case, applied the match, even while the victim protested his innocence.

The cut which is here given is the exact reproduction of the photograph taken at the scene of the lynching at Clanton, Alabama, August, 1891. The cause for which the man was hanged is given in the words of the mob which were written on the back of the photo-

SCENE OF LYNCHING AT CLANTON, ALABAMA, AUG. 1891.

FAC-SIMILE OF BACK OF PHOTOGRAPH.

graph, and they are also given. This photograph was sent to Judge A. W. Tourgee, of Mayville, N.Y.

In some of these cases the mob affects to believe in the Negro's guilt. The world is told that the white woman in the case identifies him or the prisoner "confesses." But in the lynching which took place in Barnwell County, South Carolina, April 24, 1893, the mob's victim, John Peterson escaped and placed himself under Governor Tillman's protection; not only did he declare his innocence, but offered to prove an alibi, by white witnesses. Before his witnesses could be brought, the mob arrived at the Governor's mansion and demanded the prisoner. He was given up, and although the white woman in the case said he was *not* the man, he was hanged 24 hours after, and over a thousand bullets fired into his body, on the declaration that "a crime had been committed and some one had to hang for it."

The lynching of C. J. Miller, at Bardwell, Kentucky, July 7, 1893, was on the same principle. Two white girls were found murdered near their home on the

morning of July 5th; their bodies were horribly mutilated. Although their father had been instrumental in
the prosecution and conviction of one of his white
neighbors for murder, that was not considered as a
motive. A hue and cry was raised that some Negro
had committed rape and murder, and a search was
immediately begun for a Negro. A bloodhound was
put on the trail which he followed to the river and into
the boat of a fisherman named Gordon. This fisherman said he had rowed a white man, or a very fair
mulatto across the river at six o'clock the evening
before. The bloodhound was carried across the river,
took up the trail on the Missouri side, and ran about
two hundred yards to the cottage of a white farmer,
and there lay down refusing to go further.

Meanwhile a strange Negro had been arrested in
Sikestown, Missouri, and the authorities telegraphed
that fact to Bardwell, Kentucky. The sheriff, without
requisition, escorted the prisoner to the Kentucky side
and turned him over to the authorities who accompanied the mob. The prisoner was a man with dark

brown skin; he said his name was Miller and that he had never been in Kentucky. The fisherman who had said the man he rowed over was white, when told by the sheriff that he would be held responsible as knowing the guilty man, if he failed to identify the prisoner, said Miller was the man. The mob wished to burn him then, about ten o'clock in the morning, but Mr. Ray, the father of the girls, with great difficulty urged them to wait till three o'clock that afternoon. Confident of his innocence, Miller remained cool, while hundreds of drunken, heavily armed men raged about him. He said: "My name is C. J. Miller, I am from Springfield, Ill., my wife lives at 716 North Second Street. I am here among you to-day looked upon as one of the most brutal men before the people. I stand here surrounded by men who are excited; men who are not willing to let the law take its course, and as far as the law is concerned, I have committed no crime, and certainly no crime gross enough to deprive me of my life or liberty to walk upon the green earth. I had some rings which I bought in Bismarck of a Jew peddler. I paid him

$4.50 for them. I left Springfield on the first day of July and came to Alton. From Alton I went to East St. Louis, from there to Jefferson Barracks, thence to Desoto, thence to Bismarck; and to Piedmont, thence to Poplar Bluff, thence to Hoxie, to Jonesboro, and then on a local freight to Malden, from there to Sikeston. On the 5th day of July, the day I was supposed to have committed the offense, I was at Bismarck."

Failing in any way to connect Miller with the crime, the mob decided to give him the benefit of the doubt and *hang, instead of burn him*, as was first intended. At 3 o'clock, the hour set for the execution, the mob rushed into the jail, tore off Miller's clothing and tied his shirt around his loins. Some one said the rope was "a white man's death," and a log-chain nearly a hundred feet in length, weighing nearly a hundred pounds was placed about his neck. He was led through the street in that condition and hanged to a telegraph pole. After a photograph of him was taken as he hung, his fingers and toes cut off, and his body otherwise horribly mutilated, it was burned to ashes.

This was done within twelve hours after Miller was taken prisoner. Since his death, his assertions regarding his movements have been proven true. But the mob refused the necessary time for investigation.

No more appropriate close for this chapter can be given than an editorial quotation from that most consistent and outspoken journal the *Inter-Ocean*. Commenting on the many barbarous lynchings of these two months (June and July) in its issue of August 5th, 1893 it says:

> "So long as it is known that there is one charge against a man which calls for no investigation before taking his life there will be mean men seeking revenge ready to make that charge. Such a condition would soon destroy all law. It would not be tolerated for a day by white men. But the Negroes have been so patient under all their trials that men who no longer feel that they can safely shoot a Negro for attempting to exercise his right as a citizen at the polls are ready to trump up any other charge that will

give them the excuse for their crime. It is a singular coincidence that as public sentiment has been hurled against political murders there has been a corresponding increase in lynchings on the charge of attacking white women. The lynchings are conducted in much the same way that they were by the Ku Klux Klans when Negroes were mobbed for attempting to vote. The one great difference is in the cause which the mob assigns for its action.

The real need is for a public sentiment in favor of enforcing the law and giving every man, white and black, a fair hearing before the lawful tribunals. If the plan suggested by the Charleston *News and Courier* will do this let it be done at once. No one wants to shield a fiend guilty of these brutal attacks upon unprotected women. But the Negro has as good a right to a fair trial as the white man, and the South will not be free from these horrible crimes of mob law so long as the better class of citizens try to find excuse for recognizing Judge Lynch."

REFLECTIONS
OF A WOMAN WHO GREW UP IN THE PATH OF A FAMOUS ANCESTOR

By Michelle Duster

During my early childhood years, I had a vague idea that I had a famous ancestor named Ida B. Wells, who, in my young mind "did something important to help Black people." I had more immediate concerns than to think about what a woman who was born a century before me had experienced. I spent my early childhood riding my bike, skateboarding, playing basketball, baseball, baking cookies and playing with dolls.

From the time that I was about two years old, until around the age of seven, most of the white girls who I called friends moved away one by one. I had no idea what was going on at the time, but looking back I realize it was "white flight." The neighborhood gradually transformed from a predominately white neighborhood to a predominately black neighborhood. The three remaining white neighbors during my childhood were an older couple who lived next door and a man who lived three houses down the street.

My two brothers, friends and I were Black children living in a middle class black neighborhood on the South Side of Chicago. We attended public schools in the city, rode public transportation and interacted with people from all walks of life. We knew that racism existed, but it didn't create terror in our worlds. About a dozen kids lived on the block and we all played together. The most important thing to us was having fun.

Life was unfair if we didn't get to stay out as late as we wanted. Or we got angry because we couldn't go around the block without permission. We argued with each other over who cheated in a board game, or if we claimed "cobs" (meaning they had to share) on someone's candy before they said "no cobs," which according to neighborhood law meant they did not have to share. In retrospect, I'm amazed that my parents managed to provide such a fun, carefree childhood.

We slowly became aware of the fact that we weren't welcome in Cicero, Marquette Park, Bridgeport, Ford City and a few other Chicago neighborhoods because of the color of our skin. My parents navigated our childhood so that the worst racial infractions I can remember experiencing were having a salesclerk ignore us or follow us around a store. The fact that we were living in a neighborhood that put us in limited contact with hostile whites helped create a community of people with a similar work ethic, value of education and determination to give their children opportunities they didn't have.

My parents, as well as the parents of my friends, put a high value on education, constantly telling us that "education was something no one could take away from us." I actually enjoyed school, and after fifth grade attended schools that were designed to attract top level students from a wide variety of ethnicities. The grammar school I attended from sixth through eighth grade was a magnet school that attracted students from all over the city.

I made friends with children from other neighborhoods who came from different racial, ethnic and religious backgrounds. We managed to find something in common with each other, although we lived in different neighborhoods and sometimes our parents didn't like our friendships. In addition, being a child who was curious about the world, I took the opportunity that was available through the *Big Blue Marble* television program that came on public television, and got some pen pals from other countries. I exchanged letters with girls my age from Norway and England when I was about twelve years old. As a result of these experiences, I found that we all had more in common than not.

As a teenager, I watched television in awe of the scenes of rocks being thrown at buses of Black students in Boston as desegregation efforts took place during the 1970s. I attended Whitney Young High School, which was one of the first magnet high schools to draw top level students from a variety of ethnicities from all over the city. Even in the racially segregated city of Chicago, I managed to have a peaceful, pleasant experience interacting with students who were from different neighborhoods, different racial and religious backgrounds. Throughout high school, I excelled and ended up with the opportunity to attend an Ivy League institution.

In the early 1980s, while attending Dartmouth College, I experienced hostility based on my race and gender for the first time in my life. Some students, faculty and even more so, some alumni had a problem with me being either Black, female or both. The school, which had been all-male for over 200 years, was still going through adjustments after only nine years of co-education. Some older alumni were convinced that women had "ruined the school." I was slightly unprepared for the resistance I encountered because it was my first experience being in the minority. In my previous school experiences it was not considered unfathomable for a Black person to be smart, talented and rank in the top 5% of their class, which I had achieved.

The subtle implication and sometimes blatant accusations that affirmative action was the one and only reason I got into an Ivy League institution was challenging for me to deal with at times. There was the implication that the school had to let in some Black students due to pressure, so begrudgingly they let in some Blacks even though we were perceived to be subpar in intelligence and ability. Some even implied that we had taken the place of more deserving white students. They insisted that we got special treatment.

It was the first time in my life that my right to be somewhere had ever been questioned. I had assumed that my college years would be as harmonious as the years I had spent in grammar and high school. After all, I had the good fortune of making and keeping very good friends from all races throughout my childhood. To me it was normal to interact with and befriend people from different backgrounds. And it was normal for

African Americans to be in leadership positions. The principal of my racially diverse high school was a Black man, and my teachers represented a multitude of ethnicities.

I marveled at how some older white men found nothing wrong with a scenario where only people who looked like them had the opportunity to compete. They seemed to believe it was the natural order of things for fair competition to be systematically eliminated, which ultimately ensured that only white men could be at the top.

Now, so many years after graduating from the Ivy League school where I was accused of not being qualified to attend, it would be interesting to know what explanation some of those same naysayers have in their heads to justify the undeniable fact that I earned my degree. After all, affirmative action did not take my classes for me, write any papers for me or take any of my exams. Even though I was accused of being unqualified to get in, through focus and hard work, I managed to complete four years of classes and graduate along side some of the people who had a problem with me being there.

As a descendant of Ida B. Wells, I probably grew up with the same level of stubbornness, independent will and opinionated stance on things as she. When contemplating a career path, I was determined to pave my own way through life. I didn't want my only accomplishment to be that I was related to Ida. My interest in being involved in creating positive and realistic images of the African American experience started soon after college. I started my career in advertising, studied documentary filmmaking and subsequently spent years working in marketing. In 1988, when I was 25 years old, I had the opportunity to work with New York-based documentary filmmaker, William Greaves, on a PBS film about Ida's life: *Ida B. Wells: A Passion for Justice.*

The city of Memphis had decided to make Beale Street Baptist Church – the church that Ida attended, and where she had her printing press – into a landmark. I was part of a small crew that went to Memphis to record the dedication ceremony. While working on the film, I kept a journal to record my thoughts and experiences. Below are excerpts from the journal entries I made while in Memphis from July 15 – 18, 1988.

This is my first time in Memphis and I have to say that it's a very moving experience. It's very mystical and almost creepy going into the places where Ida B. Wells went and seeing the places where horrible things happened while she was alive. It makes it so much easier to imagine what life must have been like while she was alive. This city is filled with the history of slavery and it's very moving to feel the incredible tension and spirit of this city.

Yesterday, when we were at Beale Street they had me speak to a group of children after introducing me and clapping for me. I couldn't think of anything to say. I told them something like I hope Ida B. Wells inspires them and I'm really glad that they are studying her because she was a person who could help us all.

Then today at City Hall they were introducing members of the family. At the mayor's office they had me say something which I didn't want to do. I finally said "I'm glad that the city who ran Ida out of town is finally accepting her 50 years after she died. It's a little late, but at least it's happening."

They were probably all stunned by that. I don't know if it was appropriate, but I don't care. This city is doing all of this stuff for Ida while they still have a statue of Nathan Bedford Forrest in the middle of the city. He was a founder of the KKK and a huge slave trader and breeder. There's going to be a huge celebration for him tomorrow, the day after there's a dedication to Ida. The mayor is supposed to be at both affairs. Now what type of stuff is that?

We went to the field where Ida's three friends

were killed and I was told that it looks exactly as it did when Ida was alive. It was really creepy because I could just see the men being tortured there. That place feels like a cemetery or something.

I appreciate the fact that Ida B. Wells is finally getting her respect and appreciation that she deserves, but I don't like being put on display because I'm one of her descendants. I didn't have anything to do with the fact that she was a very good writer and activist. I'm proud of her for that, but I can't take credit for it and I really don't want to get her glory. I want to get glory for something I do, not what my ancestors did.

I want to make my own name. I want to do my own thing in life. I don't want to follow someone else's footsteps, I want to create my own. That's what I told a woman today. I told her that I am making my own path. The best thing that anyone has said so far out of all of the interviews is John DeMott saying "The brightest star shines in the darkest night." He said that the extreme oppression of the day gave Ida the opportunity to have that fighter part of her come out. He said that what happened at Valley Forge made the people who were there be the way they were.

I am very happy that the city can finally pay homage to a woman who lived and worked here in the best interest of mankind. And I hope that everyone can do more than marvel at her. I hope they can be inspired by her to do whatever they can, to make this world a better place. Everyone doesn't have to be a leader, but everyone can at least do their part in helping at least one person and that person can be themselves.

During my maturation from early adulthood to my forties, I began to consider what it really means to be a descendant of Ida B. Wells. One day it hit me that I was born 101 years after her. How similar or different are our experiences? What was she about that has been passed down through the generations and therefore is a part of who I am?

Ida was born in Holly Springs, Mississippi in 1862, three years before slavery ended. Her early childhood years were filled with the hope that came during the Reconstruction period, quickly followed by the terror created by the backlash against the newfound freedom and slight economic rising of Black people.

My early childhood years took place right in the middle of the Civil Rights Movement. I was born in Chicago, Illinois in 1963 one month after President Kennedy was assassinated, two years before Malcolm X was assassinated, five years before Martin Luther King, Jr. was assassinated and riots broke out across this country. Chicago's South and West sides still bear the scars of abandoned buildings and empty lots that are remnants of those riots 40 years ago in 1968.

Each generation has had its own set of challenges and struggles. Ida's daughter, Alfreda (my grandmother), was one of the few Blacks to attend the University of Chicago during the 1920s. She was not allowed to be a member of the school sports teams, including field hockey, because of her ethnicity. My father, Donald Duster (Alfreda's son), attended the University of Illinois in Champaign-Urbana during the early 1950s where Blacks couldn't live or get their hair cut on campus. He also served in the United States Army, yet told me about a time when he was in Texas and had to sit on the back of a bus while in full uniform. My mother came of age in an all-black town in the South. Her reality when outside of the town was separate water fountains, Blacks relegated to the back of the bus and attending "separate, but unequal" seg-regated schools that many times used books that were discarded by the white schools.

Through all of these barriers, my family prevailed and instilled a sense of pride in who I am and confi-dence that anything out here in the world is available to me – as long as I got my education.

While growing up, my brothers and I learned that

some white people don't want to see us get ahead. We learned to not give people an easy reason to eliminate us. We heard the mantra that we "had to be twice as good to get half as far" as white men in particular. Our parents' experience was that a Black person had to have at least a master's degree in order to be considered for the same job as a white male with some college.

Education was something that was definitely passed down as a value through the generations. We were taught that education is something that no one can take away from us. There's no way I can be the fourth generation of college-educated people in my family without it being something that was considered important.

We were taught to be proud of who we are, and to treat others with respect. We learned to not be intimidated by anyone, but also never to look down on anyone. In addition, the responsibility to help others in whatever way we can was strongly emphasized.

The acquisition of material things has not been a

strong focus in our family. Ida lost so much due to fires and vandalism, so I assume she decided to not define herself by her possessions – that sentiment has been passed down. I remember my Aunt Ida (Ida B. Wells' daughter) constantly saying "You can't take it with you" in reference to material things. All she ever wanted was for us to give her flowers while she could smell them.

There have been many books written about Ida B. Wells, in addition to a 25 cents U.S. Heritage postage stamp created in her honor in 1990, a post office in her hometown of Holly Springs, Mississippi dedicated in her name, the house where she grew up converted into a museum, a documentary film made about her, schools and housing communities named after her, as well as plays and staged readings created to capture her life and work. She was an intimidating person to try and live up to.

I think in some ways I distanced myself a bit from the legacy, because I needed the space to figure out who I was as a woman unto myself. It was hard to do that with constant reference to being Ida's great-granddaughter, Alfreda's granddaughter, Donald and Maxine's daughter, someone's niece, cousin, sister, etc. During a part of my adulthood I craved just being Michelle with no reference points. I spent years in New York City during my early adulthood in order to explore who I was as an individual, try different career choices and spend time with my college friends, who didn't know my family.

It's taken a certain amount of maturation on my part to get to the point where I've become curious to learn more about who Ida B. Wells really was. As I continue on my journey through womanhood, I want to know about what women before me have endured. How did they handle situations? What can I learn from them? I started to be curious about not only what Ida did in her life, but what did she actually write? I wanted to see her words, her handwriting, and get some insight into her thoughts.

Other people, who are not part of our family, have researched, reproduced, and analyzed some of Ida's work. It is really good to see the bourgeoning interest in her life and work and all of us feel grateful to see her legacy being shared with a greater audience. But I started thinking about how being related to her has affected me as a woman living in the 21st century.

Recently, my father, Donald Duster, and I went through boxes that we inherited from his mother, Alfreda M. Duster (Ida's daughter), and were amazed to find some original copies of Ida's work, one of them being *The Reason Why the Colored American is not in the World's Columbian Exposition*. To actually have the opportunity to hold in my hands an original copy of something that was written over 120 years ago was moving beyond words.

The more I have learned about Ida's life, the more I understand what motivated her courage. She lost both parents and an infant brother to yellow fever when she was sixteen years old. She inherited adult responsibilities while still a teenager, and took on the role of caring for her five younger brothers and sisters.

Three of her close friends in Memphis were

Thomas Moss, Calvin McDowell, and Henry Stewart. They were like family to her and when they were murdered – basically for being strong, enterprising Black men – that was the beginning of her crusade against lynching. She knew they were innocent and that propelled her to find out how many other innocent Black men had been unjustly murdered in cold blood in the name of disrespecting white women or not being subservient to white men. She was enraged and wanted the world to know what was really going on. Maybe some of us would have been equally affected if we walked in her shoes. I'm convinced that people react to their situations, and Ida experienced a unique set of experiences that can not be repeated.

In typing Ida's actual words from the original text, I have been struck by what an incredibly cruel world Ida experienced during her early adult years. It's hard to imagine how experiencing your close friends being dragged through the street and unceremoniously killed would affect one's view of the world.

In Ida's piece, *Class Legislation*, she mentions how

the emancipation of Black citizens was viewed by some whites as a form of punishment to them. Ten decades later, some white men viewed affirmative action programs – that gave women and minorities a chance to compete – as a personal affront that was damaging to them.

While in college I was outraged by stories that were printed in a right-wing, student-run newspaper that was distributed in the dorms on a weekly basis. Most of the stories were derogatory towards anyone who was not white, male and Christian. I'll never forget one photo that was in the paper of a Black man hanging from a tree with a caption like "The Good Ol' Days." I was disturbed by the whole sentiment and the audacity for someone to put something like that outside of my door. Almost one hundred years before, my great-grandmother Ida actually experienced her friends coming to their deaths in the form of lynching.

As different as the life experiences that Ida and I had, what struck me most while typing her words from *Lynch Law* was how much there are still some of the same struggles. Black men are still being used as scapegoats for crimes they didn't commit. I remember the almost mob-like frenzy to get the Black men who beat and raped the white, female Central Park jogger in 1989. Five Black teenage males were arrested and convicted of the crime. They served 7-11 years for a crime they didn't commit. In 2002, those five men were released after the one man who actually committed the crime was convicted.

I think about Susan Smith of South Carolina, accusing an imaginary Black man of kidnapping and killing her two children in 1994, when she in fact drowned them. I think about the unarmed West African man, Amadou Diallo, who died in 1999 from a hail of over 40 bullets fired by police in Harlem because they thought his wallet was a gun. Then, most recently in 2006, in the small town of Jena, Louisiana six Black males were arrested and originally charged with attempted murder for fighting a white male classmate, who went to a school event later that same evening. Several months later, community outrage brought attention to the contrast between the harsh treatment of the Black boys versus the lack of criminal charges brought against the white boys who were involved in earlier provocative incidents. The charges against the Black youth were later dropped or reduced.

I think about how many times my own brothers, cousins and friends have experienced blatant harassment from police because they were young Black males. For that reason only, they were viewed as "suspect" and treated in such a manner. I realize that the struggle is not over.

Black women still don't have the same experiences as white women. I have yet to see the same level of outrage when a Black woman is raped followed by the same level of frenzy to catch the perpetrators as I've seen when white women have experienced that type of violation.

I have been in the workforce for almost 25 years and have yet to see a representative number of Black women's faces sitting around a corporate conference room as I do white women. On so many occasions, I have been the only African American in the room. Yet, we're supposed to believe that equality has arrived. In corporate efforts to achieve a diverse workforce I've seen numerous cases where most of the Black men work security, the copy center, mail room, customer service and information technology while the majority of Black women are receptionists and administrative assistants. When I look at annual reports of large corporations and turn to the page featuring the Board of Directors, the great majority of the time significantly more than half of the people are white men.

Some white people refuse to recognize that they have benefited from the legacy of slavery. I realize it's difficult to admit that talent alone is not the only contributing factor to success. However, it simply isn't possible to have almost three hundred years of free labor, followed by one hundred years of law that prohibited Black people from having equal access to anything, to say that a system didn't contribute to the inequality that still exists today.

Granted, not all white people have benefited from

laws that denied Blacks the opportunity to compete. But, the millions of people who have benefited from systematic elimination of competition based soley on skin color really need to be honest with themselves. When I was working at a brokerage firm in New York City, my boss had me take care of some of his personal expenses. This was an eye-opening experience for me. He had about $25 million worth of investments that I personally saw. He had different brokerage accounts in each of his three daughter's names, plus one in his wife's name and his own. I watched how he transferred money from one account to another. He jokingly complained to me about how he would have to pay for his daughters' college educations, followed by a purchase of condos for them.

Seeing the money that was waiting for his daughters made me realize the extreme difference of our realities. I did not grow up having $6 million in my account when I was ten years old. I would guess that very few African Americans have grown up with that level of financial security. However, I assume that most of the white millionaire men at the same firm were in a position to do something similar for their children.

I grew up with a sense of pride in my heritage and emphasis on fairness and doing my best, but I graduated from college with a substantial amount of student loan debt and not one cent in my account to pay for a down payment on a condo. The people who don't have to worry about having student loans follow them for years, or think about how to come up with money to buy property have managed to avoid a burden that is placed on some people. I don't understand how one can honestly say that things are equal when one person grows up never having to worry about money or opportunity, while others are making huge sacrifices in order to get their toe in the door.

Some of my Ivy League classmates never had to think about where they were going to work after graduation. Their parents, or friends of their parents, owned or ran businesses, so only a couple of phone calls were required in order for them to have a job secured with no interview necessary. I, on the other hand, went on job interviews with the same college degree and was asked on several occasions about how many words I type per minute when I was seeking a position that would put me on a management track.

Things have improved over the past 100 years, but I am not convinced that the effects of slavery, Jim Crow laws, and insidious discrimination have been erased. I don't believe this when I still have white co-workers or associates who express fear about the idea of visiting a predominately Black neighborhood, regardless of the income or professional level of its residents. In some people's minds, most Blacks have questionable character, live in gang-infested, dysfunctional environments, and therefore need to remain separate. This warped view is not surprising given how white-owned media insists on highlighting the negative things that occur in areas that are predominately Black. In Ida's *Lynch Law* piece she talks about how most of the media outlets were owned and controlled by white Americans. 100 years later very little has changed. We have a few minority-owned media outlets, but they don't have the same far-reaching power as the white-owned media. Our stories are still mostly controlled by white editors, at white-owned stations, with white-owned distribution channels.

I don't have the same level of rage and indignation as Ida, because things have gotten better over the last 100+ years. The way that racial favoritism is manifested today is so much harder to prove. I have seen plenty of situations where a white male with less education than I possess, be taken under someone's wing and groomed for positions that he was otherwise unqualified for. By contrast, I have been told that I'm missing some elusive category of experience. This manner of playing racial favoritism is more subtle, but it exists. Only when I see African Americans with potential taken in and groomed in the same manner will I believe that things are equal. Most Blacks who are not already qualified don't have the luxury of being groomed. We have to step into the role already prepared to excel with no room for error. There are still two different measuring sticks.

I'm sure there would be many people to argue about my above statements, thereby proving how subtle exclusion based on race is today. It has been twisted into something that can easily be dismissed as a figment of our collective imaginations. Almost eighty years after Ida B. Wells died some of the top performers and earners in music, sports and acting are Black. We have Black elected officials, business owners, scientists, lawyers and a myriad of other professionals who have managed to excel. However, over 44% of the prison population is Black, while we make up 12% of the population.

At the beginning of the 21st century – over 140 years after slavery ended – disparity is still significant regarding mean household income when comparing race.

In 2005, the mean household income for households headed by persons identifying as below races was*:

Asian alone – $76,747

White alone – $65,317

Hispanic or Latino – $45,871

African American or Black – $40,685

*The U.S. Census Bureau, Current Population Survey, 2005 Annual Social and Economic Supplement

25

African Americans have progressed from being a population that had a 90% illiteracy rate and were predominately relegated to low-skilled, low-paying jobs. However, almost eight decades after Ida B. Wells' death we still have an income gap, an education gap, a home ownership gap, an incarceration gap, and an access to healthcare gap that needs to be addressed. The fact that the vast majority of corporate Board of Directors, CEOs of the Fortune 1000 companies, representatives in Congress and Senate, and the Forbes list of richest people are white and male I fail to see how total equality has been achieved. We have progressed, but there's still work to be done.

IDA B. WELLS

Ida B. Wells was born a slave in 1862 (three years before slavery ended in 1865), in Holly Springs, Mississippi. Her father, James, was a carpenter and her mother, Elizabeth, was a famous cook. Both parents were literate and taught Ida how to read at a young age. She was surrounded by political activists and grew up with a sense of hope about the possibilities of former slaves within the American society. Both parents died, along with an infant brother, during the 1878 yellow fever epidemic when Ida was 16 years old.

At that young age, she assumed the responsibility of rearing her five younger brothers and sisters.

She soon became a teacher in order to earn money for the family and eventually ended up working in Memphis. In the early 1880s, she was sitting in the ladies' coach on a train as she had on many other occasions. A new rule had been imposed which required that all Blacks sit in the unequal "colored car," which doubled as the smoking car. She refused to move on her own accord, and it took the conductor and two other men to forcibly remove her from the car. The incident humiliated and incensed Ida so much that she wrote a scathing article about her experience in her church's newspaper. The article made such an impact that it launched her journalist career. In order to further fight for her rights, Ida sued the Chesapeake & Ohio Railroad and won, only for the case to be appealed and the ruling reversed a few years later.

As injustices against former slaves raged throughout the South and a reign of terror began, Wells' sense of indignation and quest for justice was fueled. She used her pen to expose the motives behind the violence. She knew for a fact that some of the victims of lynching were innocent people. This led her to investigate the facts behind other lynchings that took place. She discovered that lynching had become one of the main tactics in the strategy to terrorize Blacks, and exposing its real purpose became the target of her crusade for justice. When three of her male friends, who were upstanding, law-abiding, successful businessmen (in direct competition with white businessmen), were lynched on the pretext of a crime they did not commit, Wells wrote about the situation with a clarity and forcefulness that riveted the attention of both Blacks and whites. Her major contention that lynchings were a systematic attempt to subordinate the Black community was incendiary.

She advocated for both an economic boycott and a mass exodus from Memphis to Oklahoma. She traveled throughout the United States and England, writing and speaking about lynching and the government's refusal to intervene to stop it. This so enraged her enemies that they destroyed her presses, and put a price on her head, threatening her life if she returned to the South. She remained in exile for almost forty years.

Wells went to Chicago in the 1890s where she met and married Ferdinand Barnett, a widower and a fellow crusader who was a well-known attorney as well as the founder of *The Conservator* newspaper. In addition to raising Barnett's two children from his previous marriage, the couple had four children of their own in eight years. Even with this added responsibility, Wells continued in her relentless fight for social justice. She was very active in the suffragist movement and became one of the founding members of the National Association for the Advancement of Colored People (NAACP) and the National Association for Colored Women (NACW).

Ida B. Wells-Barnett died in 1931, leaving a formidable legacy of undaunted courage and tenacity in the fight against racism and sexism in America.

Source: Duster, Alfreda M. (editor), *Crusade for Justice: The Autobiography of Ida B. Wells.* Chicago: University of Chicago Press, 1970.

How We're Related to Ida B. Wells-Barnett

Ida B. Wells and Ferdinand L. Barnett
had four children

1ST GENERATION

Charles Aked, Herman, Ida and Alfreda
Their youngest daughter, Alfreda Barnett,
married Benjamin Duster
Benjamin Duster and Alfreda Barnett Duster
had five children

2ND GENERATION

Benjamin Duster, Charles Duster, Donald Duster,
Alfreda Duster Ferrell, Troy Duster
These five grandchildren produced a total of
fifteen great-grandchildren

3RD GENERATION

Michelle Duster is one of those
fifteen great-grandchildren.
She is the daughter of Donald Duster.

Michelle Duster earned her bachelor's degree in Psychology from Dartmouth College in Hanover, New Hampshire and her master's degree in Communications from the New School for Social Research in New York City. An avid writer, she has spent most of her career working in advertising and marketing. A native Chicagoan, she is the great-granddaughter of Ida B. Wells.

Troy Duster is Silver Professor of Sociology and Director of the Institute for the History of the Production of Knowledge at New York University. He also holds an appointment as chancellor's professor at the University of California, Berkeley. He is the author of several books including *The Legislation of Morality* (The Free Press, 1970); *Cultural Perspectives on Biological Knowledge* (Ablex, 1984) with Karen Garrett; and *Backdoor to Eugenics* (Routledge 2003 – 2nd ed). He has written numerous articles on youth unemployment and post-industrialism, diversity and higher education. A native Chicagoan, he is the grandson of Ida B. Wells.

Note

1. Baker, Ray Stannard, *Following the Color Line: American Negro Citizenship in the Progressive Era*, New York: Harper and Row, 1964 (originally published in 1906).

References

Allen, Theodore W., *The Invention of the White Race: Racial Oppression and Social Control*, New York and London, Verso: 1994.

Giddings, Paula J., *Ida: A Sword Among Lions*, New York: Amistad (HarperCollins) 2008.

Harding, Vincent, *There is a River: The Black Struggle for Freedom in America*, New York: Vintage, 1983.

Harris, Cheryl, "Whiteness as Property" in Kimberle Crimshaw, Neil Gotanda, Gary Peller and Kendall Thomas, editors, *Critical Race Theory*, New York: The Free Press, 1995, 276-291.

Roediger, David R., *The Wages of Whiteness: Race and the Making of the American Working Class*, New York and London: Verso Press, 1991.

White, G. Edward, *Justice Oliver Wendell Holmes: Law and the Inner Self*, New York: Oxford University Press, 1993.

Also Available!

Ida
From Abroad

The timeless writings of
Ida B. Wells from
England in 1894

ISBN: 978-0-9802398-9-8

After the office of the Memphis *Free Speech* newspaper was destroyed and a price put on her head, Ida B. Wells became an exile from Memphis, Tennessee in 1892. She went to New York City where she wrote and started speaking to large groups of people about the brutal realities of lynching. She subsequently spent several weeks in the United Kingdom during 1893 speaking about these realities.

In 1894, Ida B. Wells returned to England where she continued to speak about the lawlessness in the United States. Her column, "Ida B. Wells Abroad," for the *The Daily Inter Ocean* newspaper and some personal correspondence provide a vivid picture of the challenges, triumphs, alliances and obstacles that Ida B. Wells encountered in her efforts to elicit support from the British to impact change in the United States.

Michelle Duster, great-granddaughter of Ida B. Wells, compares her life experiences to those of her great-grandmother to highlight the challenges and progress of African American women born a century apart.

CPSIA information can be obtained
at www.ICGtesting.com
Printed in the USA
FFOW01n2120020715
14856FF